Six-Word Lessons on

INFLUENCING
WITH GRACE

100 Lessons to Genuinely
Connect with Colleagues,
Friends, Family and Lovers

Nikki Rausch

Published by Pacelli Publishing
Bellevue, Washington

Six-Word Lessons on Influencing with Grace

Published by Pacelli Publishing
9905 Lake Washington Blvd. NE, #D-103
Bellevue, Washington 98004
Pacellipublishing.com

Cover and interior design by Pacelli Publishing
Cover photo by Grigor Ivanov via Deposit Photos
Author photo by Nikki Closser Photography

ISBN-10: 1-933750-36-7
ISBN-13: 978-1-933750-36-1

Introduction

Webster's dictionary defines the verb *influence* as "to move or impel a person to some action." Influencing a friend, colleague, family member or lover could take on a number of different forms. You could influence through positive messages and behaviors that cause a person to take one path over another. Unfortunately, many people take a negative or divisive perspective and influence through manipulation or deceit to get what they want. Rather than view influence as a win-win proposition, they accept (and some embrace) a win-lose proposition. If you want to genuinely connect with colleagues, friends, family members and lovers, influence must be exercised with the utmost integrity and in the spirit of win-win relationships. That is why I wrote **Six-Word Lessons on Influencing with Grace.**

In this book, you'll get 100 concise, simple-to-understand lessons to help you positively influence those you deal with day-in and day-out, as well as useful tips to understand yourself and others, communicate effectively, and genuinely connect with those you encounter and love every day.

My genuine hope is that you will glean some positive nuggets from this book and put them to use right away. I invite you to visit YourSalesMaven.com and tell me your story.

Acknowledgements

I have been blessed with wonderful teachers and mentors in my life. Three in particular who have helped shape me into the person I am today are:

Lindagail Campbell
Stacy Dore`
Russell Short

I would also like to thank the amazing people who were willing to read my first few drafts and offer feedback for improvements. I am truly grateful.

Leigh Carter
Stacy Dore`
Laurel Vaughn
Nicolette Bouw

Special thank you to Lonnie and Patty Pacelli for all your support and guidance along the way to getting this book published.

This book is dedicated to Joel. Thank you for showing me every day what it truly means to be loved.

Table of Contents

You Have Influence, Now Use It

1

Apply these lessons to all interactions.

The purpose of this book is to give you tips that will enhance and improve communication between you and the important people in your life. Many of these lessons can be applied to every interaction you have with another person. I wish you continued success in your relationships!

2

Ask yourself what you really want.

In any relationship or interaction with another person, ask yourself, "What do I want?" This simple question will give you a direction and help determine your behavior, how you approach the other person, and how you respond to him or her.

3

A personal mantra for your success

Get into a positive state of mind by having a personal mantra that you say to yourself before each interaction. Choose something that inspires you to be your best self. Being authentic and confident adds to the appeal of your message.

4

Smile and light up the room.

A friendly smile can go a long way toward building rapport. If you are someone who normally comes across as serious, try smiling more often when greeting people. Knowing when to smile and have a friendly demeanor helps put people at ease and establishes relationships quicker.

5

Learn how to say someone's name.

Our names are important to us. Take the time to learn someone's name when meeting him or her for the first time. Avoid shortening it without permission. Don't call him Chris when he introduced himself as Christopher. This can diminish rapport.

6

Create a strategy for remembering names.

Here's a simple strategy for remembering names that engages your sense of sight, sound, and touch. Imagine you see a person's name written across her forehead, then say her name out loud. Next, use micro-muscle movements to write her name on your hand using your index finger.

7

It's not what you said, it's . . .

Only a small percentage of communication is relayed through the actual words used. A larger percentage of communication comes from your voice quality, including tone and tempo. Remember the phrase, "It's not what you said but how you said it." Keep your tone in mind when delivering information.

8

Those most flexible have the influence.

In negotiations, the person with the most flexibility generally has the most influence. Seek ways to be flexible in achieving your outcome. Have a few possible alternatives ready. This will offer you an advantage when negotiating for what you want.

9

Learn how to speak her language.

Using someone's words instead of para-phrasing helps diminish the chance of a misunderstanding. To influence and make a positive impression on another person, use her exact words. If she says, "collaborate" and you say "support," it may not have the same impact and meaning to her.

10

Saying back his words invites revision.

Repeating back what someone says using his key words and phrases is a way to ensure you understand. It also lets the other person know you are listening and gives him the opportunity to revise or clarify what he said.

11

Take responsibility for the whole interaction.

Taking responsibility for how your message is received by the other person gives you the power to make adjustments when needed. If you're not getting the response you want, change what you're doing to make it easier for the other person to be more receptive.

12

Voice inflection can impact your credibility.

A voice that drops down at the end of a statement is perceived as more credible than a voice that curls up at the end of a statement. A voice that curls up may make the statement sound like a question and makes the speaker sound less sure of himself.

13

People take a poker face seriously.

To be taken seriously when presenting your ideas to another person, in addition to curling your voice down at the end of each statement, pay attention to your facial expression. When delivering facts, you're perceived as more credible with a neutral facial expression versus a big friendly smile.

14

Slow down so they can process.

When delivering information, slow down your rate of speech. This gives your listener time to process what you're saying. This is especially important if they are hearing it for the first time. When we're excited or nervous we tend to speed up, making retention less likely for the listener.

15

Beware of selling past the close.

When you get a yes from the other person in regards to buying your product or service, move on to closing the sale. People who keep going may talk themselves right out of a sale. Many times that yes can come before you're done with your whole presentation. That's okay--stop selling and take the order.

Vital Skills for Your Career Growth

16

The relationship is the top priority.

Approach interactions with others with the mindset of maintaining and improving your relationship as the primary goal. This increases your willingness to be flexible. It's not about the other person always getting her way. It's about looking for a solution so that both feel satisfied with the relationship.

17

Open questions with a softening phrase.

Two softening phrases that can be used when asking a direct question are: "I'm wondering" and "I'm curious." Your tone will play a key role here so when using these phrases ensure that you really are wondering and/or curious.

18

Tilt of the head conveys curiosity.

Your body language can reinforce nonverbally that you are curious and/or wondering. A simple way to do this is to tilt your head to one side. With a slight tilt of the head and a curious tone, just about any question can be asked in a respectful manner.

19

Give specific feedback to ensure success.

It is important to recognize people for what they do well. In order to reinforce their behavior, give specifics about what you liked or thought they did well. It means so much more than a general statement like, "Good job."

20

Feedback does not mean being critical.

When someone asks you for feedback, give him at least three specific things you thought he did well. This reinforces what he should continue doing. With his permission, offer one or two suggestions for improvement that may help in the future.

21

Feedback requests that will benefit you.

When asking someone to give you feedback, be specific in your request. Let him know what you are looking for feedback on. If he gives you feedback that is outside of your request, thank him kindly and redirect his attention to your original request.

22

Learn how to tell a story.

We learn through stories. A well-told story is something people will remember for years to come. Storytellers are leaders and have the power to influence. Learn the art of storytelling. This will give you another avenue for effective communication.

23

Many of us think in stories.

We have episodic memory--we think in stories. There is a beginning, a middle, and an end. Keep this in mind throughout your communication or presentation. Make it easy for people to understand you. Use this format when presenting new information.

24

Indirect way to make a point.

Using a story to make a point, demonstrate a concept and engage your audience allows listeners to come to their own conclusions. A meaningful and appropriate story may have more influence than all the facts and data you could supply.

25

There is power in your eyes.

In order to give people time to process information, learn to divert your gaze. If you look directly at someone while he is trying to think, you can disrupt the process. Learn when to meet people's eyes and when to respectfully divert your gaze.

26

Use your gaze
to direct attention.

If you want someone to look at your product or proposal, use the power of your own gaze to direct their attention. When your gaze and attention is focused on an object, people will follow your lead and direct their own gaze there as well.

27

A conditional close will give insight.

When appropriate, use a conditional closing question in order to tease out any hidden agendas. A conditional close question to ask someone is "If I could demonstrate to your satisfaction that XXX would be taken care of, would you be interested?"

28

What tone goes with that email?

Have you ever picked up a particular tone in an email? How can that be when there's no audio to go with it? Chances are you're either drawing on your past experience with that person or making some assumptions. Notice what happens when you make a decision to read the email in a neutral tone instead.

29

Set yourself up for email success.

Knowing that people have a tendency to add their own tone when reading emails, do all that you can to ensure your message comes across friendly and professional. Start the email on a positive note by sharing a short friendly exchange before getting down to business.

30

Please keep your professional composure intact.

There are times in business where you may need to be stern, reprimand a subordinate, or clearly redefine boundaries with a tough client. When this happens, it's important that your next encounter sends the message that you have moved on and are not holding a grudge. Demonstrate this by maintaining your professional, friendly demeanor.

You Control Your Thoughts and Emotions

31

Transform negative questions into something positive.

How many times have you asked yourself, "What's wrong?" Your brain automatically begins to search for the answer even when nothing is wrong. Change the question to, "What specifically do I want?" which will redirect your thought process toward a more positive answer.

32

Distance yourself from the negative feelings.

When you refer to something as "my" or "mine," you're claiming attachment to it. Notice the difference between using "my pain" and "the pain." Decide if the negative feeling is something you want to maintain. If not, distance yourself by thoughtfully choosing your words.

33

Be honest--is your criticism true?

When you catch yourself uttering negative comments about yourself, stop and ask, "Is this true?" If the answer is no, it's time to replace your inner dialogue with something more realistic. If the answer is yes, then decide if you want to make changes.

34

Make friends with your inner critic.

Learning to look for the positive intent behind your inner critic's commentary may hold the key to what is stopping you from getting what you want. Try asking your inner critic, "What is your positive intention for me right now?"

35

Become aware of your limiting beliefs.

A limiting belief is usually caused by some part of us that's feeling hopeless, helpless or worthless in some way. Identify which of the three categories your own limiting belief stems from by noticing the internal dialogue you're using to reinforce this limiting belief.

36

Transform hopelessness into what is possible.

Hopelessness is a limiting belief of thinking something you desire is not possible. Turn this belief around by asking yourself, "What resources would I need for this to be possible?" Make a list of ways you might obtain these resources.

37

Learn to do what they do.

Believing others are capable of something you're not leaves you with a limiting belief of helplessness. The key to turning help-lessness around is gaining a greater understanding of how others do what they do. Once you know how they think and behave, you can incorporate similar thoughts and behaviors into your own life.

38

Letting go of beliefs of worthlessness

Feeling that you don't belong or don't deserve success may stem from a limiting belief of worthlessness. To help you let go of these feelings, create a list of ten things you do well. This will start the process of recognizing and appreciating your true value.

39

Mental block? Get up and move.

When you find yourself in a negative state of mind, get up and move. Remaining still will inevitably lead to retention of your bad mood or negative feelings. Taking even a short walk around the room will allow for new thoughts and new feelings to emerge.

40

Setting realistic goals to ensure success.

When setting a new goal for yourself, do all that you can to ensure your own success. First, set a goal where the outcome is within your control. Next, assign a specific time frame for completion. Last, make the goal a manageable and achievable size.

41

Goals that are within your control.

Since we cannot control someone else's behavior, it is important to set goals that are directly managed and controlled by the person setting the goal. Think about what specific action(s) you need to take in order to accomplish your goal.

42

Include a time frame for accomplishment.

Assigning a time frame to your goal allows you to track your progress. If you decide you're going to work out three times per week or make that important call today by 5 p.m., you now have a yardstick to measure how you're doing.

43

How do you eat an elephant?

Answer: one bite at a time. Each goal should have only one objective. If your goal has the word "and" in it, you have multiple "bites" or objectives. To ensure your success, pick one and accomplish it first before moving on to the next objective.

44

Answer these questions before committing yourself.

Before making commitments to others, make sure you answer "yes" to these questions: "Is this something I want to do?"; "Is this something I can do?"; "Is this something I have time to do?"; "Is this something I will do?" Maintain healthy boundaries in your relationships by only committing to what works for you in your life right now.

Revel in Your Committed Loving Relationship

45

How do you know you're loved?

Do you know you're loved when you're told so, when you see the nice things your partner does for you, and/or experience physical touch? Get clear on what lets you know you're loved and communicate that to your partner.

46

How does your partner experience love?

Crucial information can be found by asking your partner this question, "What lets you know that I love you?" Actively listen to what he or she has to say. The answer will give you a roadmap of how to continue to express your love.

47

Focus your attention on what works.

Spend time thinking about the things your partner does or says that make you feel more loving toward him or her. We naturally tend to search for what's wrong or what's not working. Instead, spend time noticing and acknowledging the things you want more of in your relationship.

48

Tell your partner what you appreciate.

Verbalize your appreciation and be specific so your partner is clear on what he is doing that is making you happy. Put a little extra effort into communicating how much you appreciate his actions. Acknowledging the behavior will encourage it to continue.

49

When should you bring it up?

There are times in a loving relationship when you might feel irritated at your partner. Before bringing it to his or her attention, ask yourself, "Will I remember this two weeks from now?" If the answer is "no," develop a strategy that respects your feelings and let it go.

50

Letting go of the little things.

A quick strategy for letting go is to imagine the incident captured in a photo. As you imagine looking at the photo, drain the color out of it, make the photo the size of a stamp, and place it across the room. This lets you disassociate from the incident and makes it easier to let go of it.

51

When to apologize and ask forgiveness.

When you feel you have made a mistake or behaved poorly, recognize your misstep and apologize immediately. Verbalize to your loved one the reason for the apology and ask for forgiveness. Going above and beyond the simple "I'm sorry" shows respect to your partner and your relationship.

52

Unsure of what to do next?

After you've apologized and asked for forgiveness, there may be more required to mend the situation. If you're not sure of next steps, ask your partner. A statement such as, "I know this requires more from me to mend this situation. I'm unsure of what to do next. I'm curious, what would you suggest?"

53

When disagreeing avoid "always" and "never."

The statements made when using words like "always" and "never" are typically finite and often inaccurate. Generalizations like these may put people on the defensive, and could pit you against your partner. Instead, give specific examples to illustrate your point of view.

54

You only have control over yourself.

Relationships develop patterns. For example: she leaves her towel on the floor so I hang it up, and because I hang it up, she leaves it on the floor--thus creating a pattern. To change outdated or negative patterns, do something different. Your behavior change may initiate a new behavior in your partner, and result in a more satisfying pattern.

55

How have I sustained the behavior?

Instead of trying to change your partner's behavior, ask yourself, "What have I been doing that has sustained the behavior?" Becoming aware and taking responsibility for your actions gives you the opportunity to make the necessary changes to your own behavior.

56

Use imagination to create new behavior.

Imagine your partner acting in the way you desire. How would you behave differently toward him or her as a result? Begin acting and responding "as if" your partner had already made the desired behavior changes. Notice the subtle shifts that start to occur in your interactions.

57

Exhale to offer release when tense.

Many people hold their breath when they are tense or upset. When you find yourself in a tense situation, exhale. This sends your body a nonverbal message to start breathing regularly again. An added benefit of your exhale is that it may encourage the other person to do the same.

58

Strengthen your foundation with sincere appreciation.

Saying "please" and "thank you" to your loving partner communicates respect and courtesy. These simple phrases may make the difference in how your request is received by your partner. Being consistent in your sincere appreciation for your partner strengthens the foundation from which your relationship can continue to grow and evolve.

Relish Your Time Spent with Family

59

Tell him what you really want.

Instead of saying, "Don't leave your clothes on the floor," tell him specifically what you want him to do, such as, "Please hang your clothes up in the closet." This simple switch will significantly increase your chances of getting the behavior you do want.

60

Put yourself on the same level.

Imagine what it is like to have someone stand over you when you're seated and literally "talk down" to you. How likely are you to really listen to what she has to say? Keep this in mind when talking to a child. Put yourself at their eye level to deliver your message.

61

That button is out of order.

A negative pattern may emerge once your family knows your "hot buttons" and how you react when they're "pushed." Disrupt the pattern by doing something out of character or unusual. Becoming unpredictable may give your family pause the next time a similar situation arises.

62

"Just kidding" can leave lasting impressions.

In families, teasing can create an atmosphere of fun and laughter. However, negative comments that go along with the phrase, "just kidding" may be internalized and become a limiting belief for the person hearing it. Choose your words with care.

63

Be heard without raising your voice.

When emotions are running high, there can be a tendency to raise your voice in order to be heard. Instead of engaging in a yelling match, try lowering your voice as you continue to talk. The other person will either have to stop talking or lower her voice in order to hear what you're saying so she can respond.

64

Gain new insight with three perspectives.

Additional insight can be found by learning how to look at your interactions from three different perspectives. The first perspective is self, your own point of view. The second is other, the person with whom you're interacting. The last is observer, an impartial perspective.

65

Looking out through your own eyes.

When you think back to an earlier situation involving a family member, it's important to learn how to view it from all three perspectives. Start by imagining stepping into your own shoes and looking out through your own eyes as you replay the earlier situation. What new awareness is revealed?

66

Stepping into shoes of the "other."

Next, replay the situation by imagining stepping into the shoes of the "other" person. Notice what it's like to interact with you. Observe the tone, facial expressions, and language the other person experiences when talking with you. How is it for them to communicate with you?

67

Take on the role of "observer."

Lastly, imagine being an impartial observer of the interaction between you and the other person. As the "observer," become aware what each person is doing and saying that's enhancing their communication. Notice what each person is doing and saying that is diminishing their rapport and contributing to the breakdown in communication.

68

The art of shifting between perspectives.

Learning how to shift easily between all three perspectives allows for continuous feedback in your interactions with family members. Use your new insight to make adjustments to your own behavior to ensure positive encounters with the important people in your life.

69

Specifics provide understanding of an experience.

When someone makes a general statement about her day--perhaps about an occurrence or conversation--ask for more information. Some key phrases to try are: what specifically, how specifically, and who specifically. This will lead to greater understanding of the other person's experience.

70

Perception of being a mind reader.

Being a mind reader is the equivalent of knowing what someone is thinking or feeling. People are less likely to communicate with someone who acts as if he already has all the answers. Use your listening skills and ask questions to communicate that you are open to hearing about the other person's feelings and experiences.

71

Third option beats all or nothing.

When people think in terms of "all or nothing," they may feel they have no choices. Brainstorm with your family members about alternate ways to get what they want. Having a third option to "all or nothing" gives them flexibility in their thinking and in their behavior.

72

Turn a "limitation" into a resource.

Many people have personality traits that they view as limitations. Help them reframe those "limitations" by working together to come up with times when that behavior is useful. Turning perceived limitations into resources allows them to view themselves in more positive ways.

Experience Deeper Connections in Your Friendships

73

Did we just agree to something?

Misunderstandings can arise when two people have different ideas of what an "agreement" entails. Making a simple statement like "Let's get together for coffee" may constitute an agreement for one person, whereas the other person may not give that comment a second thought.

74

Get specific to ensure time together.

When it's important to you to spend time with your friend, get specific. Set a date, a time and a place where you will meet. Without these agreed upon details, other commitments and responsibilities will continue to take precedence over actually getting together.

75

Ask this question to elicit information.

A powerful question to ask a friend is, "What else haven't you told me yet that you want me to know right now?" This opens the lines of communication so that they may steer the conversation to share with you what they really want you to know.

76

Show restraint and learn to wait.

People tend to pause at times to formulate questions, remarks or answers. If you rush through these pauses and begin talking, you may change the course of the conversation. Learn to wait; allow others time to think and finish speaking before you jump in.

77

Talk "with" instead of talking "at."

Good conversation happens when there is a smooth back and forth dialogue. That means leaving time and space for the other person to contribute to the conversation and ask questions. Without this, people may feel you're talking "at" them rather than talking "with" them.

78

Ask permission before giving your advice.

When a friend comes to you with a problem, many of us feel compelled to tell him what he "should" do. Instead, ask if he would like your advice or if he prefers that you just listen. This demonstrates respect for his wishes and the friendship.

79

Don't rob her of her experience.

Learn how to eliminate disclaimers from your language. For instance, when having a friend over, don't start out by saying your house is a mess. Leave those disclaimers unspoken and focus on enjoying your time together. Chances are she might never notice or care about the state of your house.

80

How do they recall their information?

One indicator of how someone processes information is by watching her eye movement. She may tend to think in terms that are visual, auditory, or kinesthetic. Once you detect the pattern, you can begin to tailor your language to support her preference.

81

Visual thinkers tend to look up.

People who process information visually tend to look up. When their eyes go up, they are either creating or recalling a picture in their mind. To engage a visual thinker, use descriptive language for how things look. Paint a picture with your words.

82

Auditory thinkers look to the side.

People who process information using their auditory sense tend to look to the side when creating or recalling data. Auditory thinkers may not need to make eye contact to be engaged in a conversation. To relate to an auditory thinker, use words that relate to how things sound.

83

Kinesthetic thinkers look down for answers.

A good indicator of a kinesthetic thinker is the act of looking down before answering a question. Looking down allows them to get in touch with how they feel about something. Using descriptive language for things like texture, feel or temperature may make the conversation more engaging for kinesthetic thinkers.

84

Help them find their own answers.

When people say, "I don't know," try offering a list of possible options. Speak slowly as you list options. The purpose isn't for them to necessarily select an option you have offered, it's to allow their minds time to sort and provide them with their own answers.

85

Have difficult conversations face to face.

When difficult conversations need to take place, have them face to face whenever possible. This allows you to notice how he is receiving and responding to what you have to say. You can then use this information to tailor your own behavior as appropriate to maintain your important friendship.

86

Not sure you want to answer.

A simple response when a friend asks you for information you're not sure you want to share is, "What makes you ask?" This gives both parties an opportunity to be clear on what they're asking and why. Based on the response, you can then decide how to proceed.

Everyday Essentials that Make the Difference

87

We each have our own reasons.

Approaching interactions with the mindset that people have their own reasons for doing what they do allows you to keep an open mind about the other person's behavior. People are more likely to communicate with you when they are comfortable being themselves without fear of being judged.

88

A strategy for responding to criticism.

Each of us have felt criticized by someone at some point. Having a strategy prepared will increase your options for how you respond to the other person's idea or opinions. Learn how to respond in a way that respects your feelings as well as the other person's while maintaining your self-esteem.

89

Do you agree with her criticism?

When someone criticizes you, it's important to first decide if you agree with what has been said. If you find that some part of it is valid, then you can apologize and take steps to handle things differently in the future.

90

You are unsure about his criticism.

There will be times when you are unsure if you agree with the criticism given. When that happens, thank the other person for his opinion. If appropriate, let him know that you would like to take some time to think it over before responding.

91

When you know it's not true.

When you receive criticism that you know isn't valid, let the person know that you've heard what he said and that you respectfully disagree with his opinion. Be cognizant of your tone and body language when delivering this message in order to maintain the relationship.

92

Don't negate your statement with "but."

When you say for instance, "I agree with you, but . . . ," you're negating the first part of that statement. Instead, rephrase with, "I agree with you, and . . . ." Start to notice where you can replace the word "but" with "and" to deliver a more positive response.

93

Being in sync takes less effort.

In physics, being in sync is known as entrainment. It takes more energy to be out of sync than to be in sync. Look for opportunities in your interactions where you can be in sync with the other person. Spend less energy and make your communication more meaningful.

94

Break the habit of conversational listening.

Many people do what is known as "conversational listening"--spending the time you should be actively listening running through possible scenarios in your mind about what you'll say next. You're likely to miss important information and diminish rapport.

95

Active listening will improve your response.

Active listening requires paying close attention to what people say; the words they choose, how they say them, and their body language. Gather and process this information before formulating your response. This reinforces to other people that they have your complete attention.

96

Communication is more than just words.

Communication can be broken down into three important categories. 1) The words you say; 2) how you say them--your tone, pitch, rhythm and tempo; and 3) your facial expressions and body language. It's estimated that your facial expressions and body language make up more than 50 percent of how your message is communicated.

97

Tell them what you can do.

When someone makes a request for something we are unable or unwilling to do, a tendency can be to tell him all the reasons it can't be done or won't work. Instead, tell him what you can do, if anything, to accommodate his request. Leave out what you can't do.

98

Pay attention to the nonverbal cues.

People give you nonverbal cues when they have heard enough of what you have to say. Pay attention to their body language. Are they looking elsewhere, shifting in their seat, trying to politely interrupt you? If so, it's time to stop talking. You'll diminish your rapport if you ignore the signs and keep talking.

99

There is a strategy behind excellence.

Seek out people who are exceptional at something that interests you. Ask them how they do it. What do they see, hear, and feel when they are performing at their best? Their answers will begin to reveal a strategy that you can then implement for your own success.

100

It is true, "It all counts."

Everything you do counts. As you learn to pay exquisite attention to your own style of communication as well as the people around you, new information will reveal itself. Use this information to make adjustments to enhance your interactions for more fulfilling relationships.

See the entire Six-Word Lesson Series
at *6wordlessons.com*

Read more about the author at
YourSalesMaven.com